XTREME RESCUES

CHILEAN M

ACCIDENT

S.L. HAMILTON

CHILE

A&D Xtreme
An imprint of Abdo Publishing
abdobooks.com

abdobooks.com

Published by Abdo Publishing, a division of ABDO, PO Box 398166, Minneapolis, Minnesota 55439. Copyright
© 2020 by Abdo Consulting Group, Inc. International copyrights reserved in all countries. No part of this book
may be reproduced in any form without written permission from the publisher. A&D Xtreme™ is a trademark
and logo of Abdo Publishing.

Printed in the United States of America, North Mankato, MN.
092019
012020

Editor: John Hamilton
Copy Editor: Bridget O'Brien
Graphic Design: Sue Hamilton & Dorothy Toth
Cover Design: Victoria Bates
Cover Photo: Chilean Presidential Press Office
Interior Photos & Illustrations: Alamy-pgs 8-9 & 28-29;
AP-pgs 4-5, 10, 12-13, 15, 16-17, 18-19, 20-21, 24 & 30-31;
Chilean Presidential Press Office-pgs 1,14, 22-23, 25, 26, 27 & 32;
Getty Images-pgs 6-7; Reuters Pictures-pgs 2-3; Wikimedia-pg 11.

Library of Congress Control Number: 2019941926
Publisher's Cataloging-in-Publication Data

Names: Hamilton, S.L., author.
Title: Chilean mining accident / by S.L. Hamilton
Description: Minneapolis, Minnesota : Abdo Publishing, 2020 | Series: Xtreme rescues | Includes online
    resources and index.
Identifiers: ISBN 9781532190018 (lib. bdg.) | ISBN 9781644943496 (pbk.) | ISBN 9781532175862 (ebook)
Subjects: LCSH: Copiapó Mining Accident, Chile, 2010--Juvenile literature. | Mining accidents--Juvenile
    literature. | Mine rescue work--Juvenile literature. | Search and rescue operations--Juvenile literature. |
    Mine safety--Juvenile literature.
Classification: DDC 363.119622--dc23

CONTENTS

CHILEAN MINING ACCIDENT

The San Jose Mine near Copiapó, Chile, caved in on August 5, 2010. It trapped 33 men deep underground. The rescue involved equipment and people from around the world. Doctors and scientists kept the 33 men alive as miners and engineers worked the drills. The rescue turned from days to weeks to months. Teams worked tirelessly to help the miners get back to the surface.

XTREME FACT

The miners survived in temperatures of 95 degrees Fahrenheit (35°C) with a humidity level of 95%.

Before the Mine's Collapse

Many workers at the San Jose Mine complained of safety issues. The mine shut down in 2007 after a miner died, but it reopened without changes being made for safety. The mine's owners were fined 42 times for not following safety rules from 2004 until the 2010 disaster. Miners were paid high wages for working in the unsafe gold and copper mine.

An overhead view of
the San Jose Mine.

There were only 3 mine
safety inspectors in Chile's
Atacama Desert region. They had the
impossible job of inspecting 884 mines in
2010. The San Jose Mine was one of those mines.

TRAPPED!

The San Jose Mine was built like a long coil that tunneled downward. It was big enough for a huge truck to drive deep underground. At around 2 p.m. on August 5, 2010, the gold and copper mine began to shake. The miners raced to the safety of a refuge room.

Miners nearer the surface managed to get out. Those deep underground were trapped in swirling dust and dirt. For hours they waited for the rubble cloud to settle. Finally, they could see large cracks in the mine's walls, floor, and ceiling. Rocks still kept falling. They knew they were in trouble.

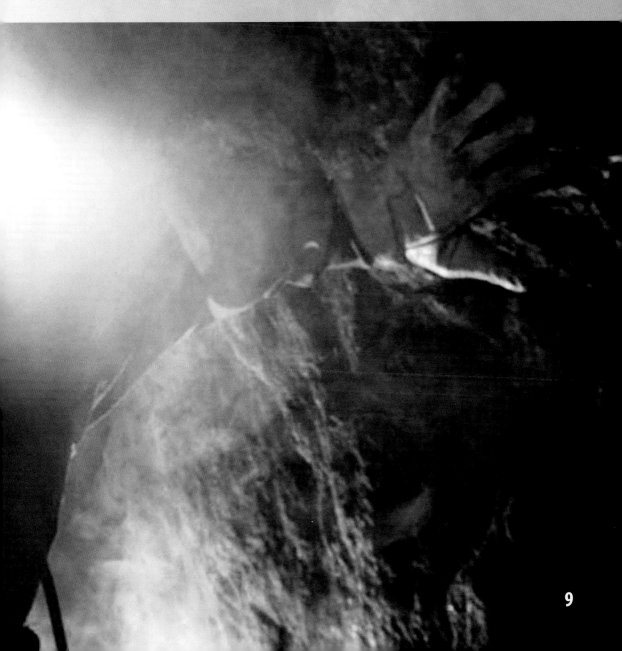

The World Finds Out

Employees of the mine tried to reach the trapped miners right after the collapse. The main tunnel spiraled down nearly one-half mile (0.8 km). Huge boulders blocked the tunnels. When they moved some rocks, others fell.

Rescue workers gather outside of the San Jose Mine on August 6, 2010.

Time was passing and all attempts to reach the lost men were unsuccessful. Rescuers instead worked on getting air shafts open. These vertical ventilation shafts linked the circling tunnels.

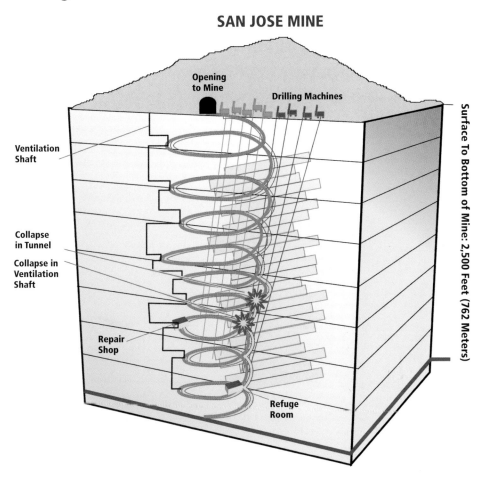

SAN JOSE MINE

News of the mine's collapse reached the world. The mine might be a grave or it might be a shelter for the missing men. No one knew if the miners were dead or alive. Was this a rescue or a recovery mission?

ARE THEY ALIVE?

Several high-speed drilling machines dug into the mine. Each machine drilled a 6-inch (15-cm) hole to a different part of the tunnel. One drill went 1,000 feet (305 m) down and another 1,660 feet (506 m). There was no sign of life. Other drills targeted the bottom of the mine where there was a safety room. It took 2.5 weeks for one drill to break into the tunnel near the refuge. At 2,250 feet (686 m) down, the rescuers waited and listened for a sign.

FIRST CONTACT

Engineers who operated the high-speed drill thought they heard vibrations coming up the drill pipe on August 22, 2010. It took 6 hours for the drill to be hauled back to the surface. They found a note taped to it:

"We are well in the refuge. The 33."

Chile's President Sebastián Piñera holds up the message the trapped miners taped to the drill to let rescuers know that they were all alive.

A camera and telephone line were lowered into the mine. The first view of the miners was seen after 17 days. The trapped miners began singing Chile's national anthem.

One of the first images of the trapped miners.

XTREME FACT

Shortly after the mine collapsed, the miners had about one-half mile (0.8 km) of tunnel they could walk through. They tried to send smoke signals to the surface by burning oil filters and tires to let people know they were alive.

PLAN A

The men were alive and rescuers knew exactly where they were. A Strata 950 drill started cutting a 15-inch (38-cm) hole down to them. According to the plan, a reamer would then enlarge the hole to 28 inches (71 cm). This would be wide enough to lower a rescue capsule. The drilling began on August 31, 2010. This effort became known as Plan A. The miners had already been trapped for 26 days. It could take 3 months to reach them.

Like astronauts, the miners were in a small area with no sunlight and limited food and air. Chile's government asked NASA for ideas to keep the men alive. The United States' space agency recommended vitamin D supplements (to replace sunlight), a liquid diet that would reduce oxygen usage, and exercises to keep the men's muscles fit and bodies ready for rescue.

An aerial view of the Strata 950, or Plan A drill.

Plan B

American Brandon Fisher had technology that could dig fast. On September 3, 2010, he and his team arrived at the mine with a Schramm T130 drill. It used compressed air to smash a drill head covered with sharpened points into the rock. This drill became Plan B.

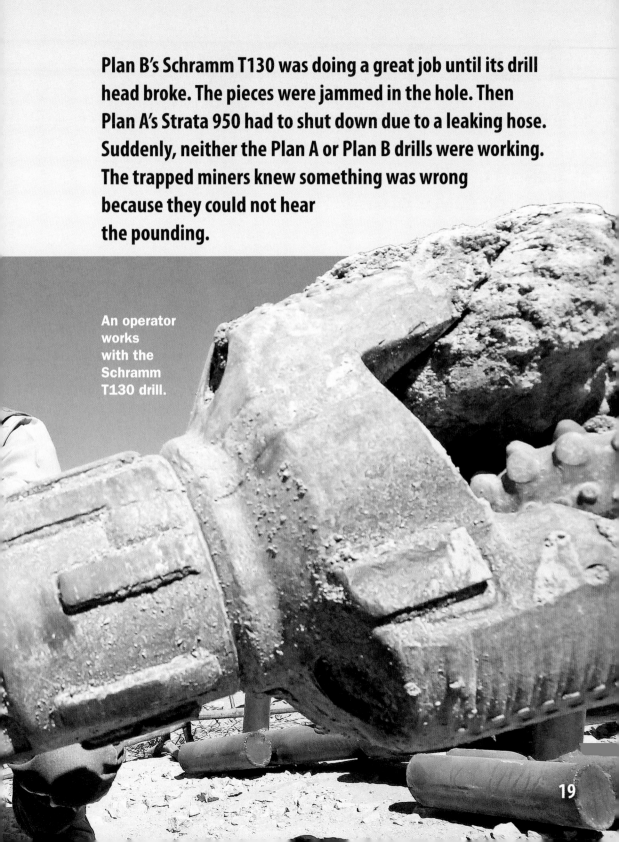

Plan B's Schramm T130 was doing a great job until its drill head broke. The pieces were jammed in the hole. Then Plan A's Strata 950 had to shut down due to a leaking hose. Suddenly, neither the Plan A or Plan B drills were working. The trapped miners knew something was wrong because they could not hear the pounding.

An operator works with the Schramm T130 drill.

Plan C

A huge drill owned by a company from Canada was stored in pieces in Bolivia. The drill's owners wanted to help the trapped miners.

Plan C's superfast Rig 421 drill stood 150 feet (46 m) tall.

The monster-sized Rig 421 drill was shipped to the San Jose Mine on 42 trucks. It arrived on day 37, becoming Plan C. The drill was constructed over nine days on a football field-sized area. It could drill 492 feet (150 m) a day. Plan C began drilling on September 22, 2010. Many people believed Plan C's huge drill would be the one to rescue the miners.

The Schramm T130, or Plan B drill, stood 42.8 feet (13 m) tall.

PLAN B AND A RESCUE CAPSULE

Plan A's drill was too slow. It was shut down. Plan C's drill was only going 50 feet (15 m) a day. It was not designed for hard rock drilling. But the broken pieces of Plan B's drill had been fished out. It was working again. It reached the miners on September 17, 2010, day 43. The next step was to use a reamer to widen the 2,068-foot (630-m) shaft from 12 inches (30 cm) to 28 inches (71 cm).

A steel rescue capsule arrived on September 25, 2010. Phoenix (*Fénix* in Spanish) was 21 inches (53 cm) wide, just big enough for one standing person. It had an intercom, video, lights, and oxygen. If it jammed in the shaft, it would split in two. The man would be hauled back down into the mine.

A Phoenix rescue capsule is tested.

PLAN B SUCCESS

The 33 miners used heavy machinery trapped with them to clear the rocks that fell from Plan B's reamer drilling. More than 20 tons (18 metric tons) dropped every day. It was dangerous work.

A banner with photos of the 33 trapped miners stood in Camp Hope.

On day 65, the drill operators talked to the trapped miners to get information. The reamer was within 10 feet (3 m) of them. They had to be careful or the tunnel could collapse. Plan B's 28-inch (71-cm) reamer finally broke through at 8:05 a.m. on October 9, 2010. It had been a total of 33 days of drilling. Three days later, on October 12, rescue worker Manuel González tested the capsule, dropping down through the shaft to the trapped miners.

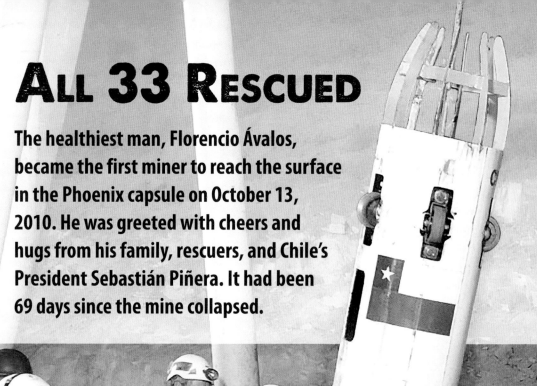

ALL 33 RESCUED

The healthiest man, Florencio Ávalos, became the first miner to reach the surface in the Phoenix capsule on October 13, 2010. He was greeted with cheers and hugs from his family, rescuers, and Chile's President Sebastián Piñera. It had been 69 days since the mine collapsed.

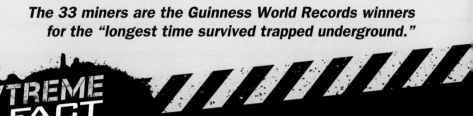

The 33 miners are the Guinness World Records winners for the "longest time survived trapped underground."

XTREME FACT

One by one, each miner was hauled to the surface. It took 9 to 18 minutes for each trip in the capsule. It rose at a rate of about 3 feet per second (1 meter per second). Every miner received a hero's welcome. The last to go was the group's leader and shift supervisor, Luis Urzúa. He was credited with saving the men's lives by gathering everyone in the refuge and rationing food.

Luis Urzúa, the last miner to go to the surface, cheered his rescue alongside Chile's President Sebastián Piñera.

WHAT IF IT HAPPENS TO YOU?

The most important factor to survive being trapped in a mine is to stay calm. Do not panic. Be sure to let other people know you are entering a mine. To help yourself survive being trapped in a mine, follow these steps:

1) Find a safe location and stay there.
2) Listen for sounds of rescuers and be ready to yell or bang on the walls to signal them.
3) Look for water.
4) Ration food.

**An average person,
if inactive, can survive
three to four weeks with only water.**

GLOSSARY

COMPRESSED AIR
Air, or a combination of air and other gases, that is under greater pressure than the air people breathe. Compressed air is often used to power machines, such as drills.

NASA (NATIONAL AERONAUTICS AND SPACE ADMINISTRATION)
A United States government space agency started in 1958. NASA's goals include space exploration and increasing people's understanding of Earth, our solar system, and the universe.

REAMER
A spinning tool that is used to widen a hole dug by a drill.

REFUGE ROOM
A strongly-built shelter used to protect people in case of an emergency. A refuge room may be stocked with food, water, first aid kits, and other supplies that can be used to help people survive.

RESCUE VS RECOVERY MISSION
A rescue mission is when a lost or injured person may still be found alive. A recovery mission is when a lost or injured person is likely to be dead, but the body still needs to be found. Sometimes search and rescue people do not know which mission they are on.

Rubble

The remains of something that has been destroyed or broken up. This often includes dirt, rocks, and building materials.

Ventilation Shaft

A tunnel that goes from the surface down into the ground to bring air to people working there. Also called an air shaft.

Vitamin D

A vitamin needed to keep the human body healthy. It is normally absorbed by the body through exposure to natural sunlight. Lack of vitamin D can cause soft, brittle bones and loose teeth.

Online Resources

Booklinks
NONFICTION NETWORK
FREE! ONLINE NONFICTION RESOURCES

To learn more about the Chilean mining accident, visit abdobooklinks.com or scan this QR code. These links are routinely monitored and updated to provide the most current information available.

INDEX